Turtles

Wendy Einstein
& Einstein Sisters

KidsWorld

What is a Turtle?

Turtles are reptiles that have a bony shell covering their whole body, except their head, tail and legs.

There are more than 350 species worldwide.

Turtles are ectothermic, or cold-blooded. This means that their body temperature is the same as their surroundings.

Turtles live alone, not in groups. But some species don't mind basking in the sun with other turtles. If there aren't enough good basking sites, turtles sometimes even pile on top of each other!

Prehistoric Turtles

Turtles are one of oldest reptile families. They have been around longer than crocodiles and snakes.

Prehistoric turtles lived about 260 million years ago (before dinosaurs existed). They didn't have a shell like modern turtles do. Instead they had special t-shaped ribs to protect their back and another set of strong ribs to protect their belly.

Modern turtles do not have teeth, but some prehistoric species did.

Archelon, an ancient sea turtle, is the largest known turtle species. It lived during the late Cretaceous period, the same time that Tyrannosaurus Rex, Triceratops and Velociraptors lived. Archelon looked a lot like today's Leatherback Sea Turtle, but it was as big as a Volkswagen Beetle.

Modern Turtles

Turtles spend most of their time in the water. This group includes freshwater turtles and sea turtles.

North American turtles are in three main groups: turtles, tortoises and terrapins.

Turtle

Tortoises live on land.

Tortoise

Terrapins live in brackish water, which is a mixture of saltwater and freshwater. Brackish water occurs where rivers and streams flow into the ocean.

Terrapin

Not everyone agrees with these three turtle groups. In Australia some freshwater turtles are called tortoises, and in Asia some are called terrapins.

Freshwater Turtle

The Turtles

The turtle group includes freshwater turtles and sea turtles.

Sea Turtle

Freshwater turtles spend much of their time in the water. They also go on land to bask in the sun or to nest.

Although freshwater turtles can be found in many different types of habitats, most species prefer shallow water that has little or no current.

Some species of freshwater turtles are not good swimmers! They walk along the bottoms of rivers, lakes or ponds instead of swimming.

Freshwater Turtles

Painted Turtle

There are many different types of freshwater turtles.

Wood Turtle

Snapping Turtle

Cooter

Slider

Box Turtle

Sea turtles spend almost their entire life in the ocean. Females go ashore only to build a nest and lay eggs. Males do not return to land after they hatch.

Sea turtles can be found in the Atlantic, Pacific and Indian oceans. They do not go into arctic waters.

Sea Turtles

Sea turtles can drink saltwater. The salt doesn't make them sick because special glands near their tear ducts take the salt out of their body. When the salt comes out of the gland, it looks like the turtles are crying.

Sea Turtle Species

Hawksbill Sea Turtle

Loggerhead Sea Turtle

There are 7 sea turtle species: Loggerhead, Leatherback, Green, Olive Ridley, Kemp's Ridley, Hawksbill and Flatback.

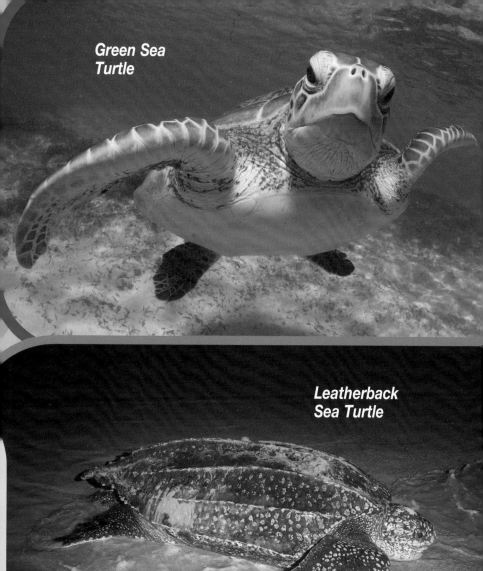

Green Sea Turtle

Leatherback Sea Turtle

The Leatherback is the largest turtle in the world.

Tortoises

Tortoises live
on land. They cannot
swim, but some species
will go into shallow
water to rest or
cool down.

*Gopher
Tortoise*

Speckled Tortoise

Most tortoise species live in deserts or semi-arid regions (places that are dry, but not as dry as deserts).

Some tortoise species live in grasslands or tropical forests.

Galapagos Tortoise

Terrapins

Because they live in brackish water, **terrapins** are found in coastal habitats. They live in salt marshes, lagoons and estuaries (where rivers meet the ocean).

The only terrapin in North America is the **Diamondback Terrapin.**

This terrapin gets its name from the diamond-shaped patterns on its shell.

The Diamondback's skin can range from white to blueish grey.

The Shell

What makes a turtle different from any other reptile? It's shell!

A turtle's shell is made of bone. It is part of the turtle's skeleton.

The shell is made up of two parts—the carapace and the plastron. The carapace is the upper part of the shell. The plastron is the bottom part.

Carapace

Plastron

Bridge

The carapace and plastron are connected by bridges. The bridges make the shell stronger and harder to crush.

Most turtles' shells are covered with scutes, a type of hard, bony scale that protects the shell.

Scutes are made of keratin, the same stuff your fingernails are made of.

Scute

Scutes

Pig-nosed Turtle

Some turtles, like softshell turtles, the Pig-nosed Turtle and the Leatherback Sea Turtle, have no scutes. Their shell is covered by thick, leathery skin.

Some turtle shells have bumps, ridges or spikes. These bumps make it difficult for a predator to grab or swallow the turtle.

Spiny Turtle

Shell Myths

Have you ever seen a turtle crawl out of its shell in cartoons?

Myth: A turtle can crawl out of its shell.
Fact: A turtle cannot crawl out of its shell. The shell is attached to the turtle.

The shell is actually the turtle's ribs, spine and breastbone.

A turtle feels pain if its shell is injured or damaged. To a turtle, a cracked shell feels the same as a broken bone feels to us.

Myth: If a turtle is on its back, it can't turn over. **Fact:** An upside-down turtle uses its head to push itself over, back onto its feet.

Hidden vs. Side-necked

Turtles are divided into two groups: hidden-necked and side-necked.

Hidden-necked turtles (called cryptodires) can pull their head straight back into the shell, so their head and neck are protected.

Hidden-necked

Side-necked

Side-necked turtles (called pleurodires) bend their neck sideways along the shell and tuck their head behind a front leg. This leaves part of their neck exposed to predators.

Snapping turtles and sea turtles belong to the cryptodire group even though they cannot pull their head into their shell.

Shell Shape

You can tell a tortoise from a turtle by the shape of its shell.

Tortoises have high, rounded shells. This shape makes it harder for a predator to grab the tortoise or crush the shell in its jaws.

Turtles and terrapins have flatter shells. A flatter shell helps the turtles swim fast and dive.

Turtle shells are also lighter than tortoise shells. Tortoises need thick, heavy shells to protect them from predators. Turtles need lighter shells so they don't sink in the water.

Feet/ Flippers

Not all turtle feet are created the same.

Tortoises' have short, stumpy legs and rounded feet. Their legs and feet look a lot like those of an elephant.

Freshwater turtles have webbed feet with long claws. Webbed feet help the turtles swim. The long claws help them climb onto logs or other surfaces to bask in the sun.

Because they spend most of their lives in the ocean, sea turtles have flippers instead of feet. The front flippers act like underwater wings, pulling the turtle through the water. The back flippers are for steering and digging nests.

Eyesight

Turtles have good eyesight. They can see what is in front of them, but they can't see much of their surroundings. Their shell gets in the way.

Turtles can see color. Some species can see more than others. Most freshwater turtles and tortoises can see red, yellow, orange and ultraviolet.

Sea turtles can see blue, green and yellow better than red or orange.

Sea turtles have great vision underwater, but with their head out of the water, they can't see very well. Think about how well you can see underwater. That is about how well sea turtles can see in the air.

The Snout

Turtles and tortoises have a great sense of smell. Sea turtles can even smell underwater!

A turtle's nostrils are near the tip of its snout. This lets the turtle hide underwater with only its nostrils sticking out so it can breathe.

Turtles and tortoises do not have teeth. Instead they have a beak. Carnivorous (meat-eating) species have a beak with a sharp, pointed tip for tearing up their prey.

The beak of plant-eating tortoises and turtles has a bumpy, saw-like edge to help grip and cut through vegetation.

Camouflage

The color or pattern of a turtle's shell can provide camouflage to help the turtle hide from potential attackers.

Some turtles have bumps or ridges on their shells that also help disguise them from predators.

Matamata

But not all turtles camouflage to stay safe. Some turtles, like the Matamata, use their camouflage to sneak up on their prey.

Snapping Turtle

Algae that grows on snapping turtle shells lets them blend in to their surroundings as they walk along a stream bottom, looking for prey.

What Turtles Eat

Most freshwater turtles are omnivores, meaning they eat plants and animals. Depending on the species, they might eat worms, snails, insects, fish, frogs, ducklings, other turtles, grasses and fallen fruit.

African Helmeted Turtles sometimes work together to hunt larger prey, such as doves or small mammals. A group will latch onto their victim and pull it under the water, holding it there until it drowns.

Tortoises
are herbivores.
They eat mostly
grasses, leaves
and flowers.

Sea turtles
can be carnivores
or omnivores. Only
adult Green Sea Turtles
are herbivores
(hatchlings are
omnivores).

Some favorite
sea turtle foods
include crabs, jellyfish,
sponges, fish,
shrimp, seagrass
or seaweed.

What Eats Them

Even though they have a shell for protection, adult turtles are still in danger from predators.

Many creatures eat freshwater turtles, including coatis, racoons, weasels, coyotes, herons, hawks, bullfrogs and snapping turtles.

Tiger sharks are the main predator of sea turtles. Orcas sometimes eat Leatherbacks

Humans are by far the most dangerous predator for turtles. People catch and eat freshwater turtles, sea turtles and tortoises.

Other Defenses

Painted Turtle

Although they are fitted with a permanent suit of armor, turtles sometimes need other defenses to stay safe from predators.

Some species, like the Desert Tortoise and Painted Turtle, pee if a predator picks them up. When the would-be attacker gets a face full of urine, it often drops the turtle and backs off.

African Helmeted Turtle

Other turtles, like the African Helmeted Turtle and Musk Turtle (also called the Stinkpot Turtle) prefer the skunk defense. When they feel threatened, they release a nasty-smelling liquid from special glands by their legs.

Common Snapping Turtle

Biting is another great defense, and no turtle does it better than the snapping turtle. Alligator Snapping Turtles can bite a person's finger clean off. The Common Snapping Turtle's bite is not as strong, but it can still cause a lot of damage.

Surviving Winter

In tropical regions, turtles and tortoises may be active year-round. But how do they survive winter in places where the land freezes?

They **brumate**, which is the same as hibernation but for reptiles instead of mammals.

Land turtles dig down to bury themselves in loose soil. They may also burrow under fallen logs or tree roots or use abandoned mammal burrows.

Aquatic turtles brumate underwater. They dig into or rest on top of the mud at the bottom of ponds or lakes where the water doesn't freeze.

In warmer climates, some species **estivate**. Estivation is like brumation except it protects turtles from drying out in really hot weather.

Butt-breathing

Turtles need
to breathe oxygen
to live. So how does
a brumating turtle breathe
when it is underwater for
months at a time?

Through
its butt!

This type of breathing is called **cloacal** respiration.

The turtle squeezes its butt muscles to push water in and out of its **cloaca** (butt hole).

Blood vessels in the cloaca draw oxygen out of the moving water. The oxygen is absorbed into the turtle's body.

Migration

Sea turtles do not brumate, but they do migrate seasonally to warmer waters.

These turtles also migrate from nesting grounds to feeding grounds. Some species migrations can take years to complete.

Leatherbacks have the longest migration of any turtle and the second longest of any animal. Their feeding grounds can be as far north as Canada or Norway. Their breeding grounds are as far south as New Zealand or Suriname. They have even been seen in the waters off Chile.

Some Loggerhead populations nest on the beaches of Japan and then migrate to feeding grounds off the coast of California.

To understand sea turtle migration, scientists put tags or trackers on sea turtles. They can then tell how far and where the turtles go.

Nesting

All turtle babies hatch from eggs. Female turtles dig nests, usually laying their eggs in sand or soil.

Female sea turtles drag themselves across the sand with their flippers to nest on beaches. They return to the same beach where they hatched to lay their eggs.

To make nests, females use their hind legs to dig a hole, pushing the dirt to the side.

The female hangs its butt over the hole, so the eggs fall into the nest. Then she covers the eggs with dirt and flattens it with her plastron to hide the nest from predators.

Eggs

Sea turtle eggs are soft, round and rubbery. This allows the female to carry more eggs and more eggs to fit in a nest.

Soft eggs also don't break as they fall into the nest hole.

Freshwater turtles and tortoises can have hard or soft eggs, depending on the species.

The temperature of the eggs in the nest determines if the hatchlings will be male or female. For most species, cooler eggs will have male hatchlings, and warmer eggs will have females.

Many predators, including dogs, raccoons, skunks and lizards, dig up turtle eggs and eat them.

Special enclosures can be put over the nests to keep the eggs safe.

Babies!!

A turtle hatchling is born with an egg tooth, called a caruncle, to help it crack out of its egg.

It also has a yolk sac attached to its plastron. This sac gets absorbed into the body and is the hatchling's food while it is still in the nest. If the sac is damaged, the hatchling will die.

Baby freshwater
and sea turtles dig
their way out of the nest
once they hatch.

They must
then dash to the
nearest water to stay
safe from
predators.

Baby tortoises
stay in the nest for
a while after they hatch.
During this time
the yolk sac is absorbed
and the shell hardens.
They can then dig
themselves out.

At Risk

Turtles are some of the most long-lived creatures in the world, but almost half of all turtle species are at risk of disappearing because of human activity.

The oldest tortoise in the world today, an Aldabra giant tortoise named Jonathan, is more than 180 years old. His species is one of many tortoise species that may become extinct.

Freshwater turtles can live from 30 to 50 years in the wild, but the number of many species is dropping.

Of the 7 sea turtle species, 5 are endangered or critically endangered, and the other 2 are threatened.

Only 1 in 1000 hatchling sea turtles survives to become an adult.

Threats

Poaching is one of the main threats facing freshwater turtles and terrapins. Turtles are killed for food or captured from the wild for the illegal pet trade.

Climate change is also a threat. Turtles struggle if temperatures are too hot or cold, or if the there is too little or too much rain.

Many turtles get hurt or killed when they are hit by cars as they try to cross roads.

Habitat loss is also a problem. When humans destroy natural spaces to make more roads or shopping centers, we are taking away places for turtles to live.

Sea Turtle Threats

Sea turtles face many of the same threats as freshwater turtles and tortoises—poaching, climate change and habitat loss. They face other dangers as well.

Every year thousands of sea turtles die getting caught in fishing gear, including nets, lines and hooks.

Pollution is another problem. The oceans are full of garbage that can harm or kill turtles if they swallow it.

Plastic bags are especially dangerous. Floating in the ocean, they look a lot like the jellyfish many sea turtles like to eat.

Jellyfish

Plastic bag

In this photo, you can see why a sea turtle might swallow a plastic bag by mistake.

If you see a turtle trying to cross a road, help it get across safely. Pick the turtle up by its shell and move it in the direction it was heading. Do not pick a turtle up by its tail. You can damage its spine.

How You Can Help

Don't litter. Put garbage in its place.

Avoid using single-use plastic products as much as you can. Choose reusable items instead.

Try not to disturb nesting sites. If you live in an area with turtles, try building spaces on your property where they might want to nest.

Think twice before getting a turtle for a pet. Many species live much longer in the wild than they do in captivity.

If you decide to get a turtle for a pet, get it from a reptile rescue, not a pet shop.

The Publisher: KidsWorld Books

Library and Archives Canada Cataloguing in Publication

Title: Turtles / Wendy Einstein & Einstein Sisters.
Names: Einstein, Wendy, author. | Einstein Sisters, author.
Identifiers: Canadiana (print) 20200301012 | Canadiana (ebook) 20200301020 |
ISBN 9781988183442
   (softcover) | ISBN 9781988183459 (EPUB)
Subjects: LCSH: Turtles—Juvenile literature.
Classification: LCC QL666.C5 E36 2020 | DDC j597.92—dc23

Cover Images: Front cover: From *GettyImages:* ShaneMyersPhoto.
Back cover: From *GettyImages:* Vladimir_Krupenkin, baxterdogy247, asserBadr_Beenthere.

Photo credits: From GettyImages: Alberthep, 42; alblec, 56; alexkuehni, 50; AntonyMoran, 38; arlutz73, 37; Artex67, 37; Aryfahmed, 60; baxterdogy247, 26, 27; Rejean Bedard, 10, 52; Charlotte Bleijenberg, 17; borchee, 34; brandtbolding, 43; BrianEKushner, 19; Aaron Bull, 48; Tanita Chunsiripongpann, 62; Callum W, 25; Catherine Withers-Clarke, 43; clintspencer, 35; CMP1975, 15; Colin_Davis, 12, 49; cookelma, 14; DanielHarwardt, 30; davidevison, 51; Dcwcreations, 51; DejaVu Designs, 33; Delves Photography, 39; dimitris_k, 44; Divepic, 41; Diy13, 61; Marta Muñoz Domingo, 53; Dragunov1981, 59; driftlessstudio, 10; EdwardSnow, 11; FabioVolu, 6; Nicola Geneletti, 9; Geo-K, 49; Holly Guerrio, 11; Carol Hamilton, 29; Jeffrey Hamilton, 24; irin717, 15, 55; jahmaica, 59; Jag_cz, 61; Jordan_Sears, 45; janaph, 13; JasonOndreicka, 7, 10, 18, 62; JHVEPhoto, 53; Anantha Jois, 7; LFPuntel, 14; Manakin, 4; MaximFesenko, 58; mjf795, 16; mmozzies 35; MR1805, 5; Musat, 40; nicholas_dale, 28; nndanko, 61; passion4nature, 45; petesphotography, 2; Photography by Adri, 8; pierivb, 32; polygonplanet, 63; PorqueNoStudios, 57; reptiles4all, 23; r0m0, 21; Michael Rolands, 3; ShaneMyersPhoto, 8; Simoneemanphotography, 55; Somedaygood, 54; Greg Sullavan, 31, 36; taeya18, 20; Topaz777.jpg, 22; tunaly, 57; UroshPetrovic, 21; Michelle de Villiers, 39; Vladimir_Krupenkin, 17; wrangel, 23; xbrchx, 11; YKD, 31; ymgerman, 52; Zofca, 46.

We acknowledge the financial support of the Government of Canada.
Nous reconnaissons l'appui du gouvernement du Canada.

PC: 38-1